M000159549

MY LIFE STORY SO FAR:
A Grandfather's Journal

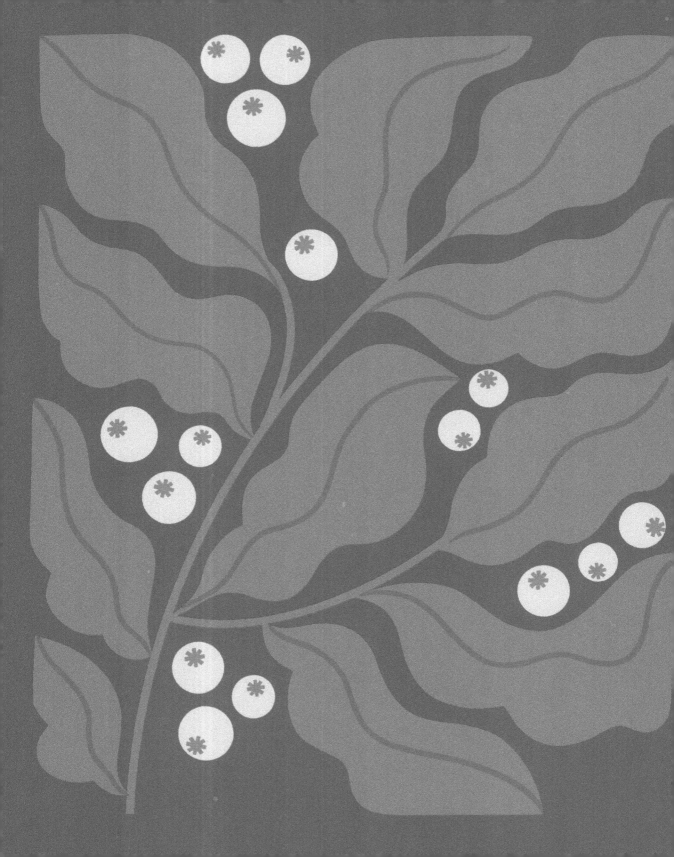

MY LIFE STORY SO FAR

A GRANDFATHER'S JOURNAL

Guided Prompts to
Write Your Own Memoir

LISA LISSON

Illustrations by Amy Blackwell

ROCKRIDGE
PRESS

For my grandparents Lester and Cecile (White) Howard
and Crafton and Anita (Carr) Talbott.

Series Designer: Heather Krakora
Interior and Cover Designer: Heather Krakora
Art Producer: Hannah Dickerson
Editor: Jesse Aylen
Production Manager: Jose Olivera
Production Editor: Melissa Edeburn

Illustrations © 2021 Amy Blackwell
Author photo courtesy of Erika Dietrick

Paperback ISBN: 978-1-63807-750-3
Hardcover ISBN: 978-1-63878-635-1
R0

THIS JOURNAL BELONGS TO

_____

BEFORE YOU START

My Life Story So Far: A Grandfather's Journal makes it enjoyable, practical, and easy to reflect on the life you've lived by writing your memoir. Once you've completed it, you'll be able to share your stories with your children, grandchildren, friends, and family.

Throughout this journal, you'll have the opportunity to delve into everything about your life that has shaped you and made you the person you are today. You will tell the stories of your early childhood and your "firsts" (first day at school, first drive, first love), and you will describe how working and raising a family changed you.

Before you start your journaling journey, read these tips to get the most out of the experience.

INSIGHTFUL AND PRACTICAL PROMPTS. Each prompt is designed to help you reflect on the life you've lived. Take your time. Let the memories come back gently without forcing them. Remember, this process is to be savored, not rushed through. You should enjoy the process of reflecting on everything that has made your life so special to you and your loved ones.

A PLACE TO BRANCH OUT. Before you begin writing, check out this book's family tree (page 4) with blank spaces for you to fill out. Take a moment to write in your own name, then think back to your parents or the people who raised you. Write down their names. Then, add the names of your own children and grandchildren. Remember, you're telling your story both to honor the people who came before you and to pass on your knowledge and stories to those who follow you.

GATHER YOUR MEMORIES. Assemble your photo albums, cards, letters, recordings, and other mementos. Review these items you've saved, and prepare to think back on the events that have made your life so meaningful and special.

ROOM TO REFLECT. In the pages ahead, you'll find ample writing space to reflect on each question. You should write to your heart's content. If you'd like to have your loved ones use this book's questions to interview you and record your answers, go ahead! There is no right way to use this journal; there's only *your* way.

Congratulations on taking the first step to writing your memoir! This journal is here to help you achieve that meaningful goal.

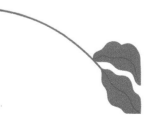

YOUR BIRTH STORY

Stories surrounding your birth likely came from your family. Perhaps a parent, sibling, or other close relative shared their memories about the circumstances of your birth. Describe the memories of those stories. Were you born at home or in a hospital? Are you named after someone? If so, who is that person and what is their relationship to you?

_____

_____

_____

_____

_____

_____

_____

_____

_____

_____

_____

_____

_____

_____

_____

_____

FAMILY NICKNAMES

Nicknames are popular in some families. Usually created by someone close to you, a nickname can be a shortened form of your own name or a completely different one. Were you given a nickname as a child or at another point in your life? What was your nickname and has it persisted throughout your life? What is the story behind your nickname(s)?

BIRTHDAY CELEBRATIONS

Birthdays are highly anticipated events in a child's life. Celebrations may be a large birthday party with friends, cake, and presents or smaller affairs celebrated with close family and perhaps a special meal. How were your childhood birthdays celebrated? What type of special food or cake was served? Pick a memorable birthday and describe your celebration, including who was present and what made it a special memory.

THE TOWN WHERE YOU GREW UP

Many people think fondly of the town where they grew up. Some grew up in the same town their entire childhood. For others, a family member's job may have required frequent moves. Where did you spend the majority of your formative years? Did you stay in the same town or even the same house? What was your favorite thing about your hometown? Perhaps your family moved around frequently. If so, describe your favorite town. What characteristics of the town made it your favorite?

THE HOME(S) WHERE YOU GREW UP

The physical homes we grow up in can be of many types and styles. The location where your family lived may have influenced the type of housing they chose, and you may have grown up in a house or in an apartment. How would you describe it? What was the general floor plan? Did you have your own bedroom? How was it decorated? Did you have a yard or other area where you played? If you moved frequently, describe the favorite house or apartment you called home.

CHILDHOOD GAMES

Games are a part of childhood. Perhaps you grew up playing tag with neighborhood friends or a game of cards with a brother or sister. Maybe you were more interested in organized sports. From board games to those created spontaneously on a summer afternoon, games are a fun part of life. What games did you play growing up? Did you enjoy sports contests, or did you prefer board games? What games do you continue to enjoy?

FRIENDSHIPS

Friends play an important part in our lives. They are with us during the fun times and support us through the difficult times. Friends share our secrets, too. Who was your best friend growing up? How did you meet? Describe the activities you did together.

A RULE FOLLOWER OR
RULE BREAKER

How would you describe your temperament as a child? Would you consider yourself mischievous, or were you a rule follower? Did you frequently get into trouble with your parents or teachers? Share a memory of a time when you got in trouble. What did you do and what were the consequences?

_____

_____

_____

_____

_____

_____

_____

_____

_____

_____

_____

_____

_____

_____

PAST GENERATIONS

Each family has its own unique story, and that family history often provides a sense of togetherness. Think back to the past generations. How many generations back can you name? What were the names of your grandparents? Your great-grandparents? Who were your aunts and uncles? Share a favorite memory or story of one or two of your ancestors.

A FAVORITE RELATIVE

Families are made up of unique individuals, but we often have a favorite relative whose visits we eagerly anticipated. Who was your favorite relative? Perhaps your favorite relative isn't a relative at all, but a close family friend. How often did you see this person? Did they live close or far away? What made them special in your eyes? Describe a favorite activity you did frequently with that person.

YOUR FAMILY'S CULINARY HERITAGE

A family's cultural heritage is reflected in the foods they eat, the language they speak, and the traditions they observe. This heritage is passed down from one generation to the next. Think back to family gatherings—which foods always show up at them? Share the origin of that food if you know it. Do some foods only appear on specific holidays? Share a memory around that dish, and include the recipe if you have it.

_____

_____

_____

_____

_____

_____

_____

_____

_____

_____

_____

_____

_____

_____

PERSONALITY TRAITS

Personality traits often run in a family. Members can be more outgoing and the "life of the party" or can be quieter and prefer an evening at home. Consider your family members. Are they a boisterous crowd when together or a more reserved, introspective group? Maybe your family is a mixture of everything in between! How is your own personality a reflection of the traits seen in your family?

YOUR FAMILY'S ORIGIN

In recent years, researching ancestors has become a popular hobby. "Where did our family come from?" is a common question among family history enthusiasts. Do you know where your family originated? Do you know the country or even the town where your ancestors lived? If you know it, share the story of how your ancestors came to be in their current homeland. Don't worry if you don't know all the facts—record what you know and the family stories you've heard.

FAMILY HEIRLOOMS

Often, mementos of family life are kept and passed from one generation to the next. These objects can range from a piece of furniture to a framed photograph or a piece of jewelry. Take a moment and walk around your home. What objects do you have that are family heirlooms? Pick one and share the story behind it. Why is that object special to your family? How did you come to possess it? What memory sparks each time you see the heirloom?

FAMILY STORIES AND LEGENDS

Every family has a family legend or funny story frequently shared at family gatherings. Maybe that story is true and maybe it's not—or maybe no one knows for sure. What is your family's legend? Which parts are true and which parts are you not quite sure are accurate?

FAMILY SAYINGS OR EXPRESSIONS

Over time, families can develop their own unique communication. These can be sayings or expressions that are often said among your family members. For example, "patience is a virtue" is a common saying in some families. Share any sayings or expressions commonly used in your family. If you know the origins of those expressions within your family, share that as well.

_____

_____

_____

_____

_____

_____

_____

_____

_____

_____

_____

_____

_____

_____

CELEBRATING HOLIDAYS

Holidays are an integral part of family life around the world, full of tradition, food, extended family, and friends. Which major holidays did your family celebrate when you were growing up? Were they faith-based holidays or fun celebrations unique to your family? Which family members or friends were usually present? Describe your favorite holiday growing up, and share why it was your favorite!

YOUR FAVORITE FOOD

Food plays an important role in families, and most people have a favorite food or two that they love to eat with their loved ones. Favorite foods are often sweets, an old family recipe, or a dish eaten out at a favorite restaurant. Describe your favorite food. On what occasion(s) and how often do you eat your favorite food? Is it sweet or savory in taste? Is it a food or dish you make yourself? If so, share the recipe.

LAUGHTER AND HUMOR

Laughter is often referred to as "the best medicine." Research shows humor is indeed good for our overall mental and physical health. Consider how humor—such as the ever-popular knock-knock jokes or funny family stories—has been a part of your life. Share the jokes that always seemed to make you laugh. Include any hilarious family stories that frequently come up at gatherings.

THE STORY BEHIND A
FAVORITE PHOTOGRAPH

Photographs are usually cherished items within a family. Whether a photograph from generations past or a photograph of a family event taken a few years ago, it tells a story. Spend some time looking through your photo albums. Pick your favorite photo and share the story behind it. Where was it taken? Who is in the photograph? Why was the photo taken? Most important, describe why the photo is your favorite and the memories it evokes. Include a copy of the photograph, if you can.

FAMILY CHORES AND RESPONSIBILITIES

Families with children frequently work together to perform a variety of daily or weekly tasks around the home. As a child or teenager, what type of chores did you perform in the home? Examples include cleaning your room, washing dishes after a meal, or mowing the lawn. Were you responsible for taking care of younger siblings or the family pet? What was your favorite (or least favorite) chore? What made it your favorite (or least favorite)?

YOUR FAMILY HOUSEHOLD

The makeup of a household can vary quite a bit and even change over time. Several generations may live under one roof, or it may be just a single parent and a child. Who were the family members living in your household as you grew up? Did you share a bedroom and, if so, with whom? What did you see as an advantage to the unique makeup of your family?

FAMILY PETS

Pets provide companionship and joy, and we often consider them family members. Cats and dogs are the most popular pets, but other animals such as hamsters, fish, and even ferrets can be beloved pets, too. Did you have a pet (or pets) growing up? If so, what type of pet(s) did you have? What were their names? Share a fond story about your favorite pet. If you didn't have a pet, what would you have liked to have had and why?

_____

_____

_____

_____

_____

_____

_____

_____

_____

_____

_____

_____

_____

YOUR SIBLINGS

Siblings have a unique bond. They share funny moments, adventures, and even fights with one another. If you have siblings, who are they? Where do you fall in the birth order? Describe the bond between you and your sibling(s) and how that bond might have changed over the years. Were you closer to one sibling in particular? Share a funny or memorable story about the two of you. If you don't have siblings, describe your relationship with someone you consider to be as close as a sibling.

YOUR FIRST DAY OF SCHOOL

The first day of school is a memorable event for any child. Preparing for the start of school often includes shopping for school supplies and new clothes. What were your feelings on your first day of school? Were you nervous or excited? Did you have a special outfit to wear? If so, can you describe it? What activities did your school day include? If you have a photo of your first day of school, include it as well.

SCHOOL DAYS

Education can take on many different forms. Think back to your early schooling and education. Describe the type of school you attended or tutoring you received. Did you have a favorite subject? What did you enjoy most about that subject? What did you enjoy least about school?

A TYPICAL SUMMER DAY

Kids often eagerly anticipate summer vacation from school. Describe a typical summer day for you as a child. Did it include playing with friends or young family members? Did you swim or play sports? Were you required to do chores or look after younger siblings? What was your favorite part of the day?

LEARNING TO DRIVE

Learning to drive can be an exciting rite of passage for some people. Do you know how to drive? If so, did you take driver's education classes or did you learn to drive from a family member? How did you feel the first time you drove a vehicle by yourself? Describe your first car. If you don't drive, was there someone who always drove you around when you were a teenager? What do you remember about their car? If you relied on public transportation, what kind(s) did you use and do you recall your first ride by yourself?

HIGHER EDUCATION

The number of students pursuing a higher degree of education beyond traditional high school has increased over the decades. Did you attend college or a trade school to further your education? If so, which institution did you attend? What was your focus of study? Share what you consider to be the most important thing you learned. Is there something you would have liked to study that you didn't?

YOUR DREAMS

As children and young adults grow up, they often dream about their future. They dream and plan their career, where they will live, and so on. Dreams and desires can change over time, but those of our childhood often hold a special place in our thoughts. What were your dreams as you grew up? Describe the person or circumstances that influenced your dreams the most. How did your dreams for your life change over time? Were you able to realize your dreams from your childhood and, if so, which ones?

RECREATION

Hobbies and sports bring enjoyment to our lives and are sources of pleasure and accomplishment, whether they are individual or group activities. What type of hobby or sport did you participate in? How did you develop your interest in it? What about that activity brought you the most joy? Share a childhood memory about your favorite recreation.

DATING LIFE

The process of finding and dating a potential spouse or partner in life has changed over the years. Many young people today use online apps to find a potential date. As you were seeking a date or spouse, how did you go about meeting someone? What type of activities did you usually do on a date? Were individual dates common or were you more likely to date in a group of people?

FIRST LOVE

Falling in love for the first time or having your first crush is an exciting time for many young people. That first love can be a brief crush, or it can turn into a forever love. Who was your first love? Did you marry that person? Describe where and how you met them and what characteristics drew you to that person.

SOCIAL ISSUES OF YOUNG ADULTHOOD

Community and world events affect our perspectives on issues, as well as how we make life decisions. For example, the state of the economy may impact where we live. As you were maturing into adulthood, what were the big issues in the local region or in the world impacting your life? Describe one issue and how it impacted your daily life or a decision you needed to make.

LEARNING SKILLS FROM OTHERS

We learn many skills throughout a lifetime. This expertise may be physical or manual skills or may be more interpersonal in nature. Often we're taught by a family member or a trusted mentor. As you grew up, what was a specific skill you learned from someone else? Describe that skill and the importance it played in your life.

_____

_____

_____

_____

_____

_____

_____

_____

_____

_____

_____

_____

_____

_____

YOUR FIRST JOB

Many people remember their first job as a way to earn extra money. For some, that first job may have been an after-school job. For others, it might have been full-time employment and a means to support themselves or help out their family. Describe your first job. What were your duties? Did you work full- or part-time? What was your favorite part of the job? Share an important lesson or skill you learned and how you continued to use it in your life.

YOUR CAREER

Your career often reflects a particular interest or skill you have, and pursuing that career over a lifetime often brings satisfying achievements. What was your career? How did you choose to pursue that career? What type of education was required to enter that field of work? Describe your responsibilities and achievements. Lastly, what was your favorite part of your workday?

YOUR WORK LIFE

Careers and work life evolve over time as interests mature and new opportunities arise. How did your employment change over time? Did you stay in the same career or line of work, or did you change your profession altogether? Think back to a work opportunity you chose to take or pass up. How did that impact your career or current job? Would you make the same choice again knowing what you know now?

JOB SKILLS

Every job and career requires a unique set of skills. Those skills may be physical skills, leadership skills, communication skills, or analytical skills. What types of skills did your job(s) require? How did you learn or develop these skills? Did you learn on the job, or did you pursue specific training courses outside your regular employment? Share an example of how you used your skills in your work.

YOUR MENTORS

A mentor is a trusted person or counselor in your life who significantly influences you. Frequently, mentors are family members, teachers, or close family friends. Did you have a mentor growing up? Who was that person and what was their relationship to you? Did they mentor you in a specific skill, or was it more life mentoring? Share your thoughts on the impact their mentoring had on you. Did you then become a similar mentor for someone else?

MILITARY SERVICE

Many people participate in military service to their country. Did you participate in military service? If so, which branch of the service did you serve in? Describe your responsibilities and duties. What type of military action did you participate in? Were you injured during your time of duty? If you didn't participate in military service, did you know someone close to you who did?

MEETING YOUR SPOUSE/PARTNER

Love is a dream many young people pursue, and they cherish the memory of meeting their love for the first time. Share the story of how you first met your spouse/partner. Was it a chance meeting or one set up by friends? What was the first thing you noticed about them? Perhaps you had known this person for years, but one day you felt the spark of attraction. Describe the time when you first realized the change in your feelings.

YOUR LOVE COMMITMENT

Committing to love and a life with a partner/spouse is an important and meaningful moment in a couple's life together. If you have or had a partner/spouse, how did you know you wanted to spend your life with them? Was it an immediate realization, or did it take some time before you knew? If you don't currently have a partner or spouse, is there someone in your life you have a great love for—perhaps a friend or relative? How do you celebrate your relationship with them?

CELEBRATING YOUR COMMITMENT OF LOVE

Ceremonies frequently mark a beginning of a couple's life together and their commitment to each other. These ceremonies/celebrations can look quite different from one couple to the next. How were romantic partnerships celebrated in your family or among your social circle? Did they follow a religious or cultural tradition? Did you observe the same traditions, or did you choose a different way to mark your commitment to your partner/spouse? Describe your celebration. Do you have a special memory from that time?

BECOMING A PARENT
FOR THE FIRST TIME

The arrival of a first child is a joyous event and brings a swirl of emotions. Share the story of your first child's arrival into the world (or your world). Was the baby born early, late, or right on time? If you adopted, what led you to that decision? Do you recall any preparations you did (or did not) complete? Describe your feelings as you became a parent and held your child for the first time.

THE STORY BEHIND YOUR CHILDREN'S NAMES

People give a lot of thought to naming a child. Baby name books list seemingly infinite options! The choice can be a topic of much discussion and contemplation. What are the full names of each of your children? Include any nicknames you might have used. How did you make the decision to name each child? Is there a special meaning to their name(s)? Were they named after anyone? If so, who? What was their relationship to you or your family?

DREAMS FOR YOUR CHILDREN

As soon as someone knows they are expecting a baby, they begin to make plans and dreams for their child. Dreams of what sport their child may play. Dreams of the type of career they may have. What type of dreams for your child(ren)'s future did you have? Why was this dream important to you as a parent? Share the dreams you had for each of your children and how those dreams may have changed over time.

SPECIAL PARENTING MOMENTS

As a parent watching your child(ren) grow and mature into young adults, you experienced many special moments and times with them. Think back through your parenting years to those poignant, funny, or happy times you spent with your child(ren). Describe a special moment you experienced as a parent. Why was that moment so special? Share why that moment continues to be a cherished memory.

FAMILY TRIPS

Many families take trips together, whether it's an afternoon at the beach, a picnic in a nearby national park, or a day at an amusement park. What type of activities did you enjoy as a family? Describe any family trips you took with your children. That trip might be small, such as getting a popsicle every year at the pier, or a larger tradition, like traveling to the same place each year on vacation.

FAMILY ILLNESS OR INJURY

Families experience many ups and downs together over time. An illness or injury of a family member can impact the whole family. Did you or a family member experience a significant illness or injury? What type of medical condition was it? Describe the process of recovery. Share how that illness or injury impacted the priorities in your life. Did you view life differently afterward? If so, how?

YOUR SPIRITUALITY

Spirituality can play a significant role in many people's lives, and traditions are often passed down through families. Not all families or individuals adhere to a spiritual belief. Was spirituality or faith important as you grew up? If not, why? If it was, did it change as you grew into adulthood? How would you describe your spirituality today? Do you continue to subscribe to the same religious or spiritual traditions of your youth? What is one belief you would share with future generations?

YOUR FAVORITE MUSIC

Music surrounds us and brings enjoyment to our lives. It can soothe you, motivate you, and help you express feelings. Hearing a favorite song can instantly spark a wonderful memory. Was music part of your life growing up? Does it continue to be an enjoyable part of your life today? What is your favorite type of music? Do you have a favorite song that instantly takes you back to a specific time and place? If so, describe that memory.

CLUBS AND SOCIAL ORGANIZATIONS

Clubs and social organizations provide a social outlet and opportunities to meet with other people with similar interests. Book clubs, gardening clubs, and bridge clubs are just a few. Are there any clubs or groups you belong to and attend regularly? What drew you to join, and what is your favorite part about attending?

LIFE GOALS

Throughout life, we are encouraged to set goals. These goals might be educational, professional, or physical. Think back to your early adulthood years. What were your goals for your life? Pick one or two of those goals and share them. What prompted you to create your goal(s)? Were they career- or family-oriented or more individual focused? Did you meet those goals, or did they change over time? Describe a large goal you met in your life.

BECOMING A GRANDPARENT

Becoming a grandparent is a special event in any parent's life. Describe the moment you learned you would become a grandparent. What were your thoughts and feelings? Describe the anticipation of waiting for your first grandchild to arrive. Share your feelings and thoughts you had when you held your grandchild for the first time.

YOUR GRANDCHILDREN

Each grandchild is a special addition to the family and represents the future generation. Share the names and birth dates (if known) of each of your grandchildren. Share something you find unique and special about each grandchild. What is one piece of advice you would like to share with your grandchild(ren) as they grow up?

SHARING ACTIVITIES WITH YOUR GRANDCHILDREN

Doing activities with a grandchild is fulfilling for both of you. Those activities can be quite simple, such as reading a book together or attending a grandchild's sporting event. Perhaps your time together is spent teaching them a new skill. Describe one or two of your favorite activities to do with your grandchild(ren). What activity do they frequently ask to do with you?

WHAT DO YOU WANT FOR
THE NEXT GENERATION?

As a grandparent, you have the unique opportunity to pass on your family's heritage and your own life wisdom to the next generation. Contemplate the lessons you have learned throughout your life. What do you consider the most important message you want to share with your grandchild(ren) and future generations?

WHAT ARE YOUR GOALS FOR THE FUTURE?

You may still be working or perhaps you've retired. Either way, as you look to the future, what are you looking forward to? Maybe you want to start a new hobby or begin traveling more. What dreams or goals are you looking forward to accomplishing? How do you plan to work on those dreams? Goals and dreams are often personal but can certainly involve family members, too. Are others included in your future goals?

YOUR CURRENT HOBBIES AND ACTIVITIES

Hobbies and pastimes offer enjoyment and relaxation, and there are so many different things to choose from. What types of hobbies or activities do you currently enjoy? Do you prefer more quiet and solitary pursuits or activities involving others that are more physically active? Share what first drew you to your current hobby or activity.

YOUR TALENTS

Everyone has a talent or two. You might have a talent for playing an instrument or telling great jokes. Or you might be great at dancing or cooking a specific cuisine. What are your talents? How did you discover you had them? How have your talents brought you joy in your life? Does anyone else in your family have these same talents?

NEW INVENTIONS

The world is constantly changing. From simple things like the paper clip to complex ones like computers, new inventions are all around us. What is one invention that had a significant impact on your life? Describe the ways in which it helped improve and change the way you live.

FAVORITE PLACES YOU HAVE VISITED

Seeing new places exposes us to new experiences and perspectives. It can be a chance to try new foods and explore new sights. Think back to the places you've visited—which ones were your favorites? Describe one of your favorite places to visit, whether it's a nearby town or a country across the world. Share what makes it a favorite. Was it the people or the experiences you encountered? Were you able to visit often?

WITNESSING HISTORICAL EVENTS

Most people remember exactly where they were when a significant historical event took place. For example, many of us remember what we were doing when the events of September 11, 2001, took place. Some have vivid memories of watching a man walk on the moon for the first time. Think back to major events you have witnessed. Choose one or two and describe what you were doing when that event occurred. What was your initial reaction? What feelings did you experience?

THE IMPACT OF LIFE CHALLENGES

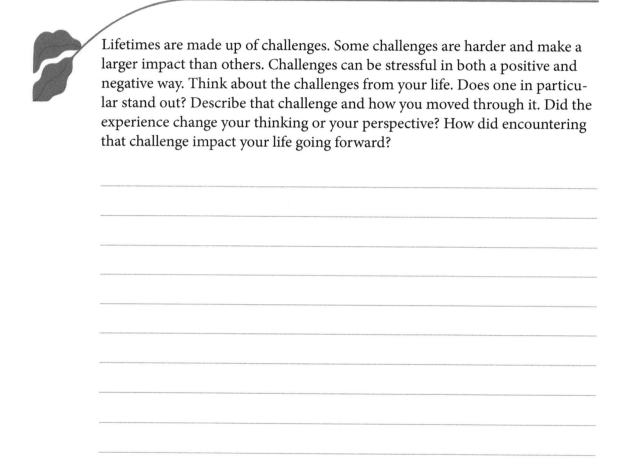

Lifetimes are made up of challenges. Some challenges are harder and make a larger impact than others. Challenges can be stressful in both a positive and negative way. Think about the challenges from your life. Does one in particular stand out? Describe that challenge and how you moved through it. Did the experience change your thinking or your perspective? How did encountering that challenge impact your life going forward?

YOUR MOST EMBARRASSING MOMENT

Life doesn't always go as planned. Almost everyone has plans that failed and resulted in sometimes embarrassing results. Looking back, describe your most embarrassing moment. What type of activity were you doing? Who were you with that witnessed your embarrassment? How did you recover your composure? Share a life lesson you learned through that incident.

YOUR AWARDS AND ACHIEVEMENTS

Receiving awards or recognitions for an achievement are special occasions throughout a lifetime. An example might be a perfect school attendance award, a top salesperson of the year award, or a significant promotion. What awards or special achievement recognition have you received in your life? Describe what receiving that acknowledgment meant to you.

_____

_____

_____

_____

_____

_____

_____

_____

_____

_____

_____

_____

_____

_____

_____

_____

A REGRET OR SOMETHING
LEFT UNDONE

Regrets over missed opportunities or something left undone in the past can bring feelings of sadness or disappointment. Words unspoken can lead to regrets, too. What is the biggest regret you have? Is it an opportunity missed? Is it a word left unsaid or a deed left undone for someone? Describe the circumstances surrounding the cause of this regret.

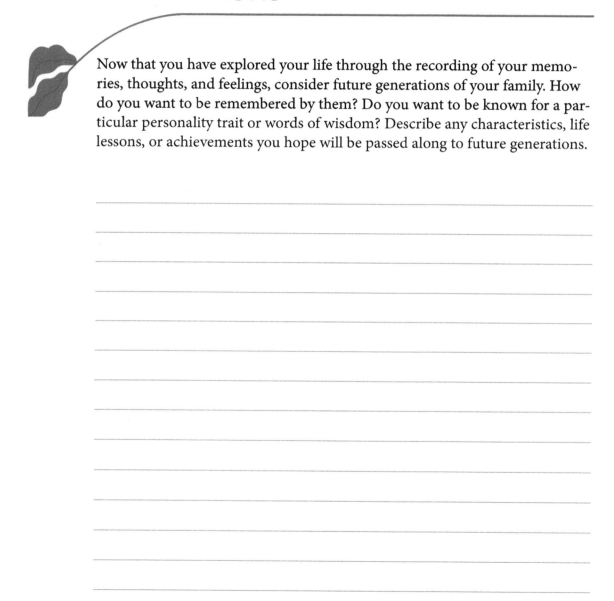

YOUR LEGACY FOR FUTURE GENERATIONS

Now that you have explored your life through the recording of your memories, thoughts, and feelings, consider future generations of your family. How do you want to be remembered by them? Do you want to be known for a particular personality trait or words of wisdom? Describe any characteristics, life lessons, or achievements you hope will be passed along to future generations.

ACKNOWLEDGMENTS

I would like to thank my husband, Bob, for his support and encouragement as I stepped out of my comfort zone to help others reflect on and share their stories. Thank you also to my many cousins who generously shared the family stories that served as my inspiration.

ABOUT THE ILLUSTRATOR

Amy Blackwell is an artist and a creative dabbler: paint, print, knit, scribble, whatever sparks her creative fancy. After graduating from university in 2007, she established an online illustration and art business. She is inspired by the weird and wonderful, clashing colors, the natural world, history, fashion, and folklore.

ABOUT THE AUTHOR

Lisa Lisson is the genealogy researcher and creator of the *Are You My Cousin?* website (lisalisson.com) and YouTube channel. She grew up attending family reunions and listening to family stories, which developed her passion for oral history. Lisa now teaches how to discover your ancestors and their stories as a local and national genealogy speaker, writer, and podcast guest. Lisa is the co-creator of *The Food Memory Project* (foodmemoryproject.com).

CPSIA information can be obtained
at www.ICGtesting.com
Printed in the USA
LVHW050445071221
705428LV00004B/4